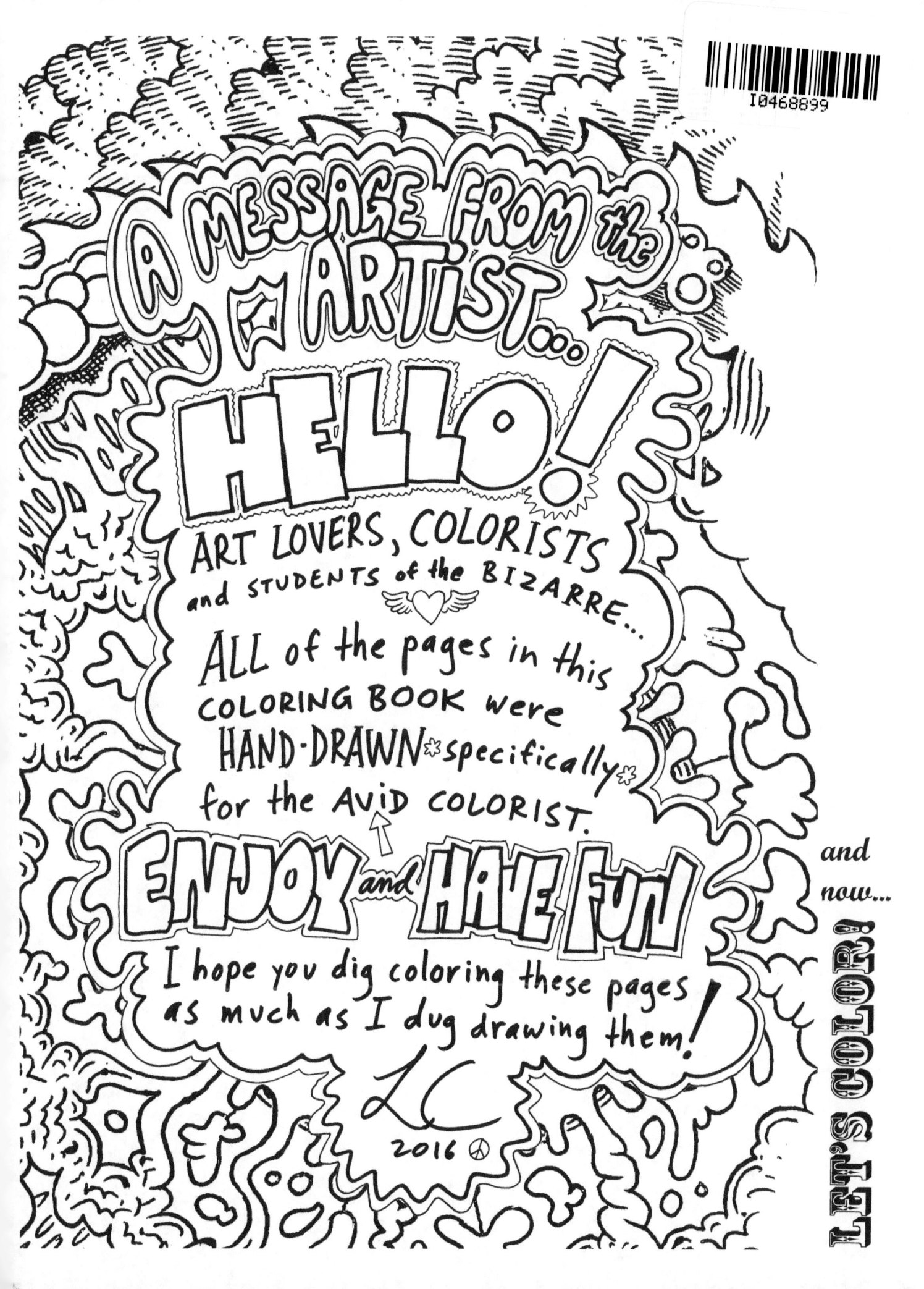

A MESSAGE FROM the ARTIST...

HELLO!

ART LOVERS, COLORISTS and STUDENTS of the BIZARRE...

ALL of the pages in this COLORING BOOK were HAND·DRAWN *specifically* for the AVID COLORIST.

ENJOY and HAVE FUN

I hope you dig coloring these pages as much as I dug drawing them!

2016

and now...

LET'S COLOR!

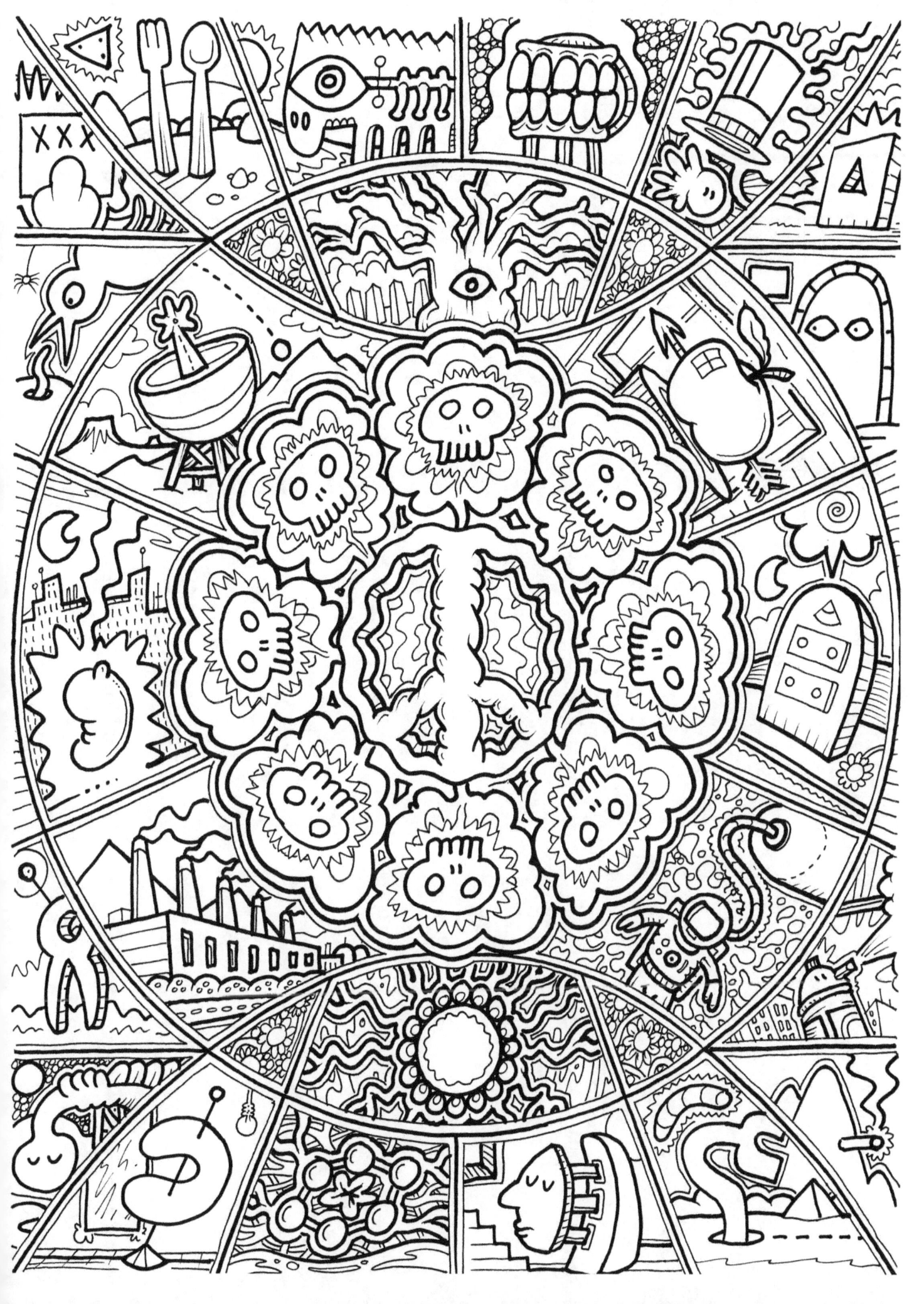

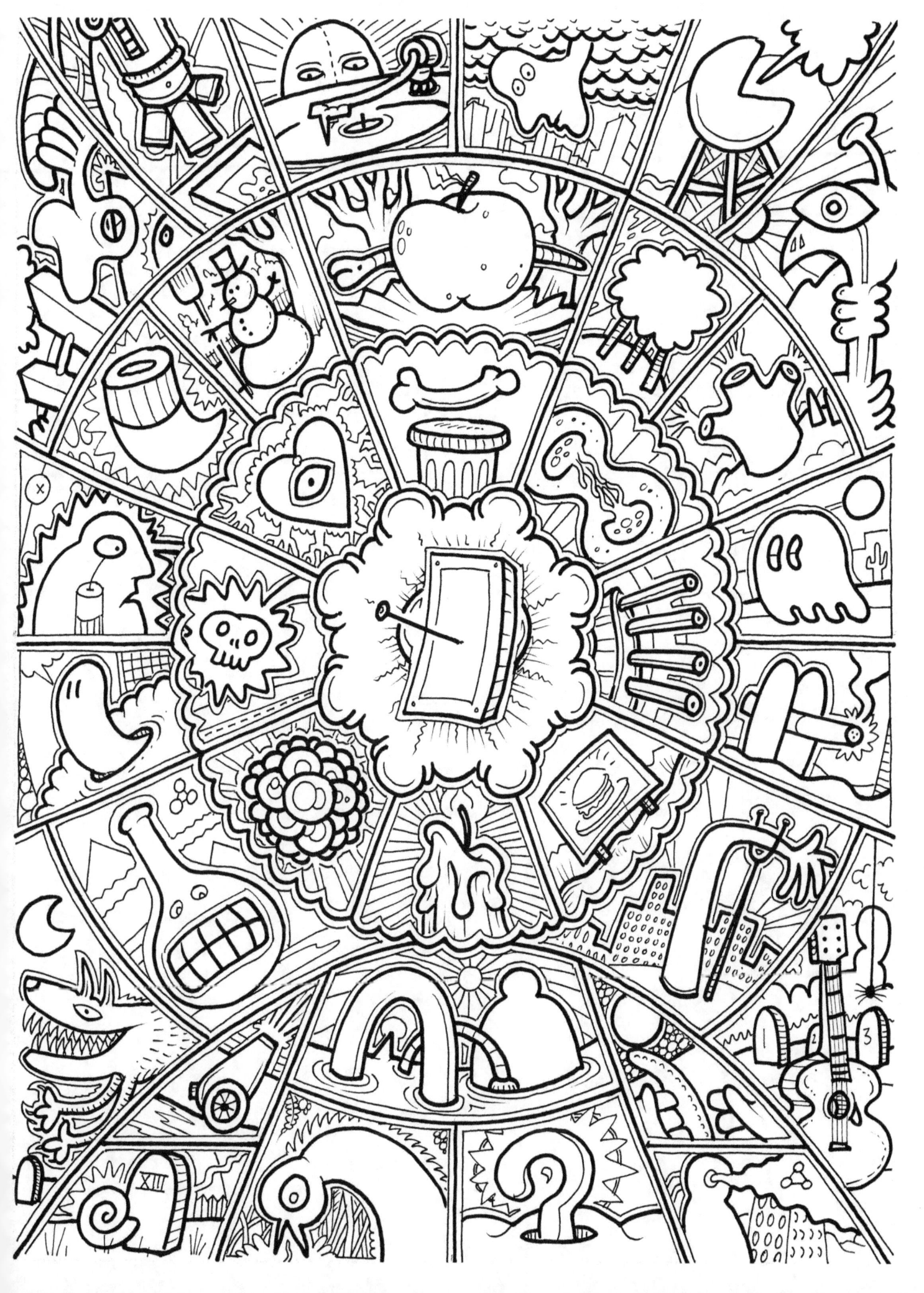

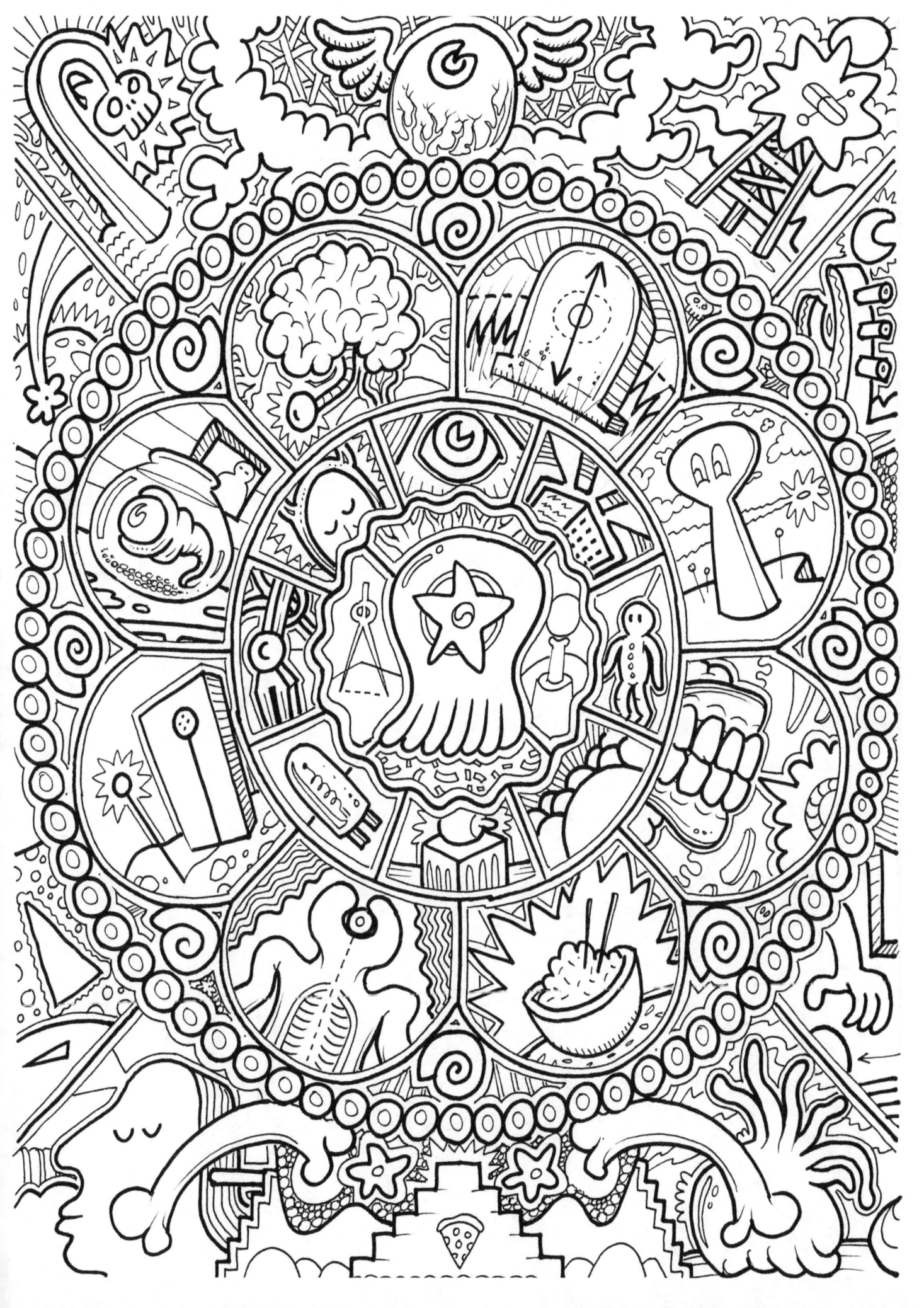

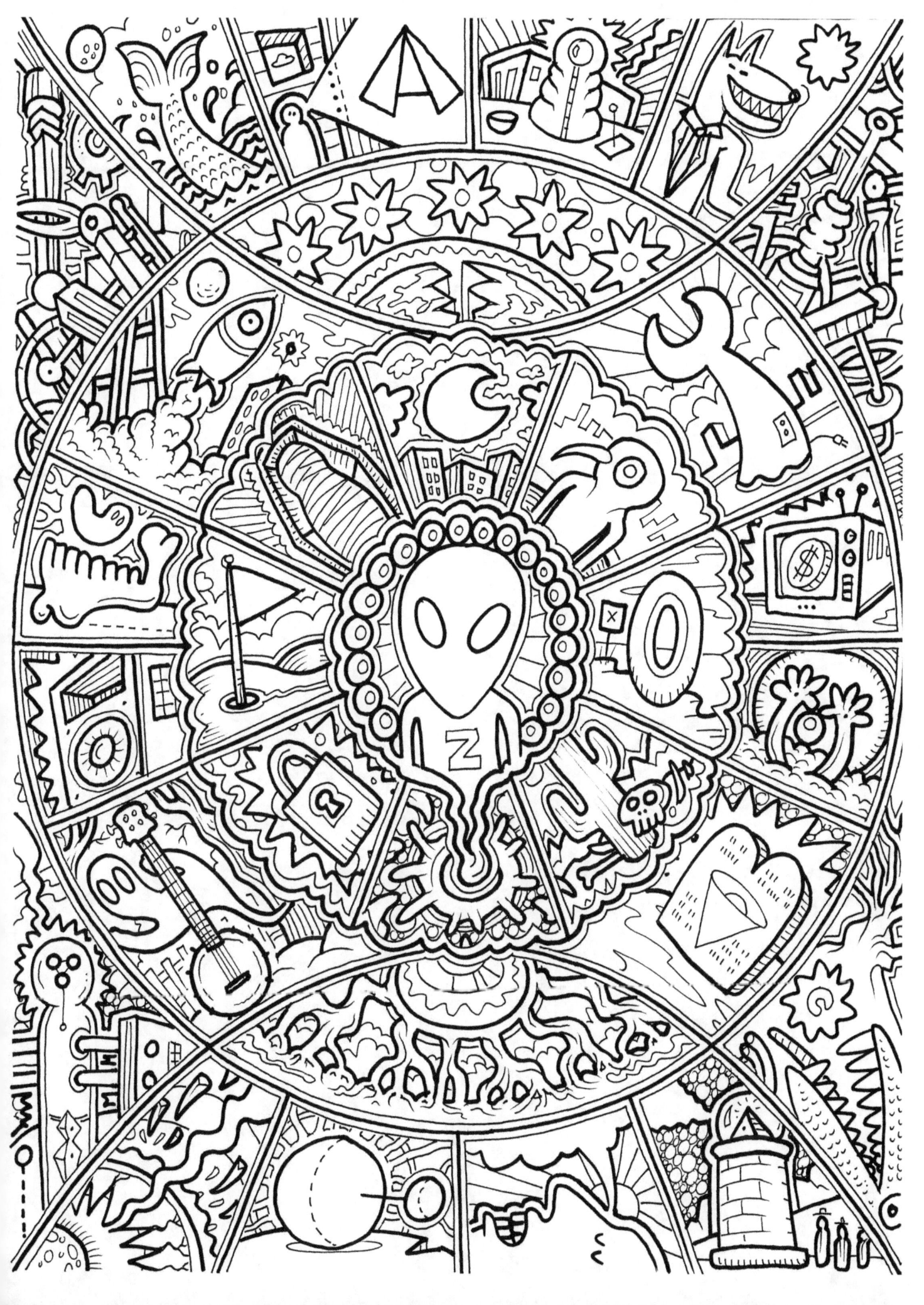

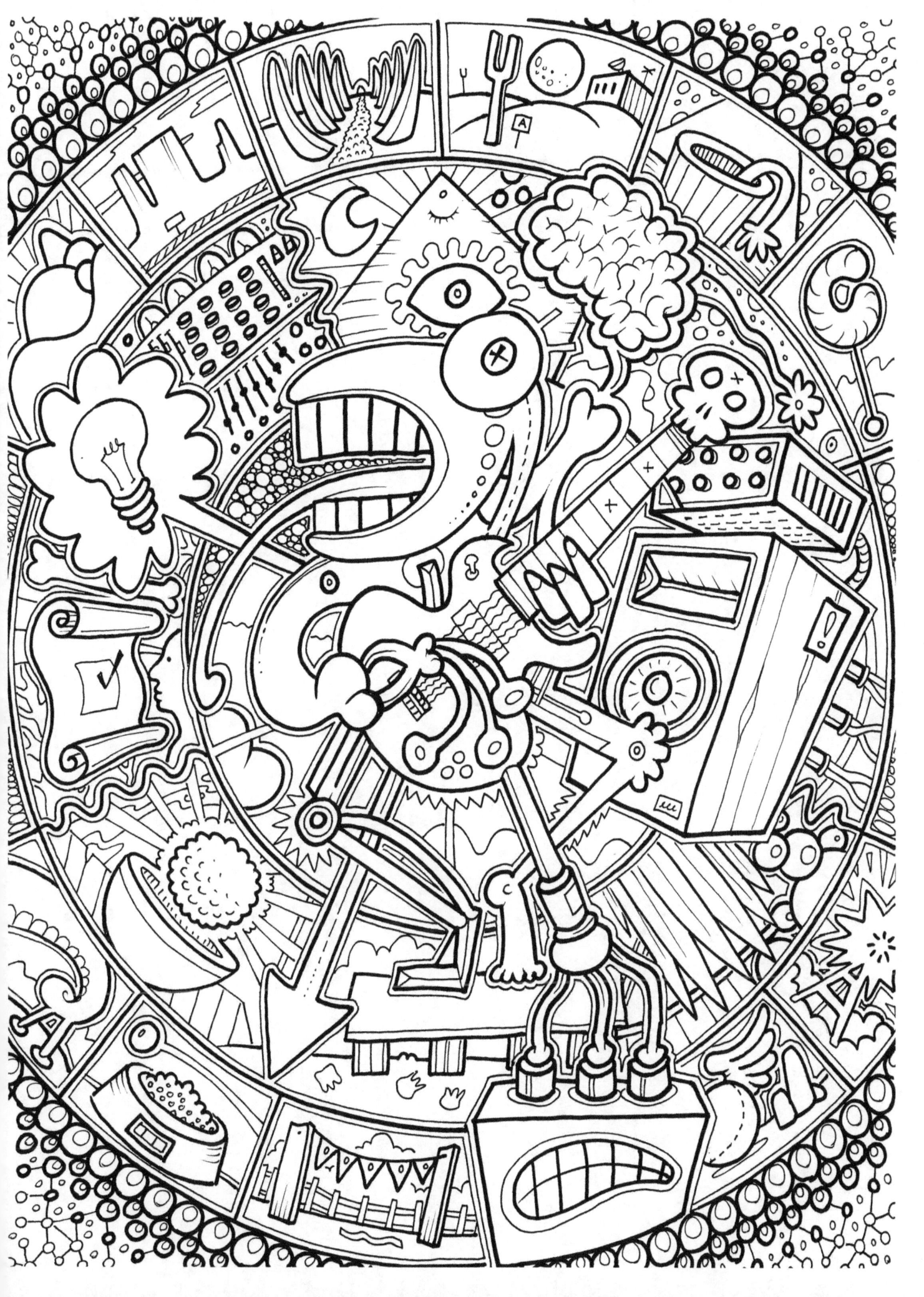

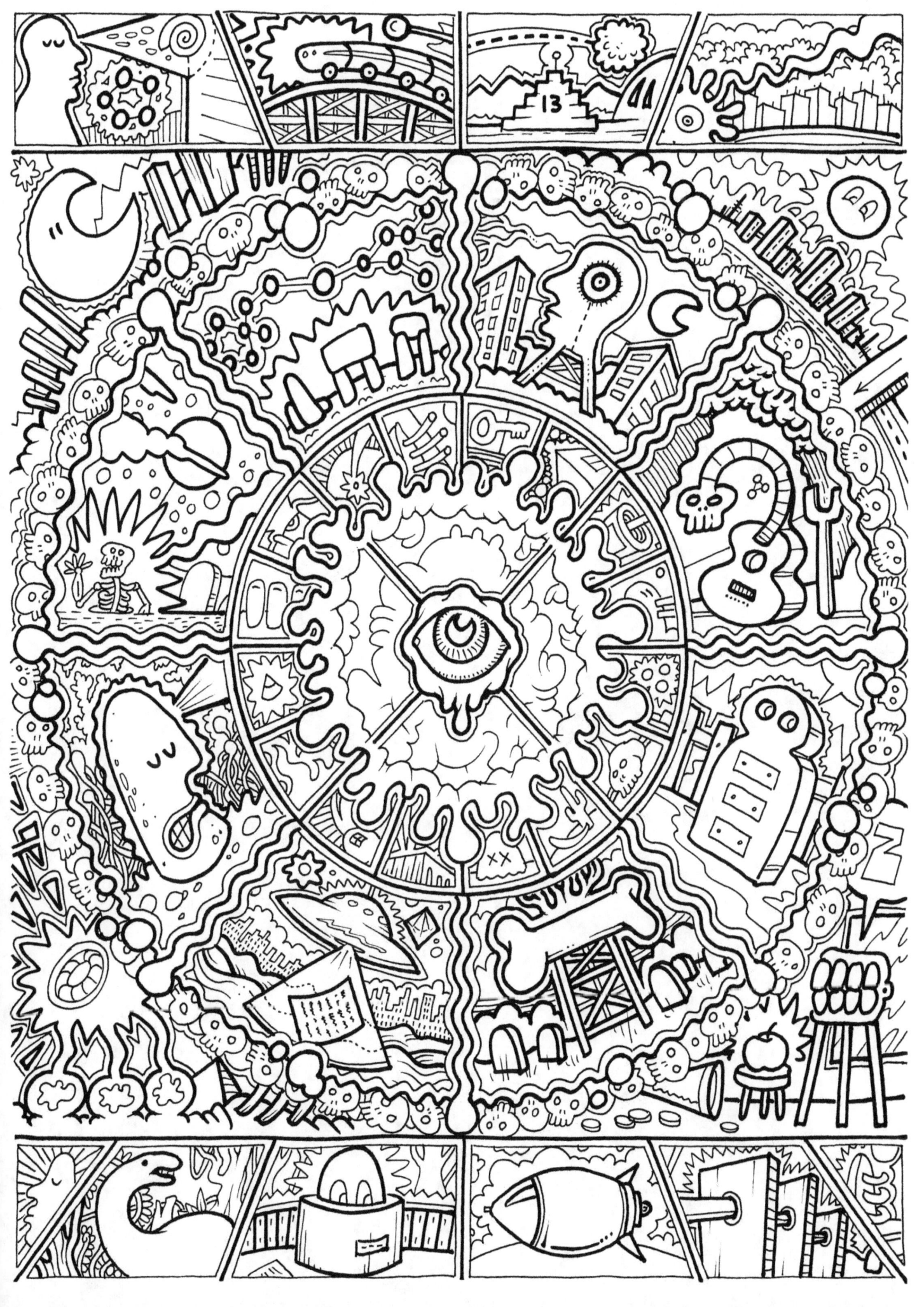

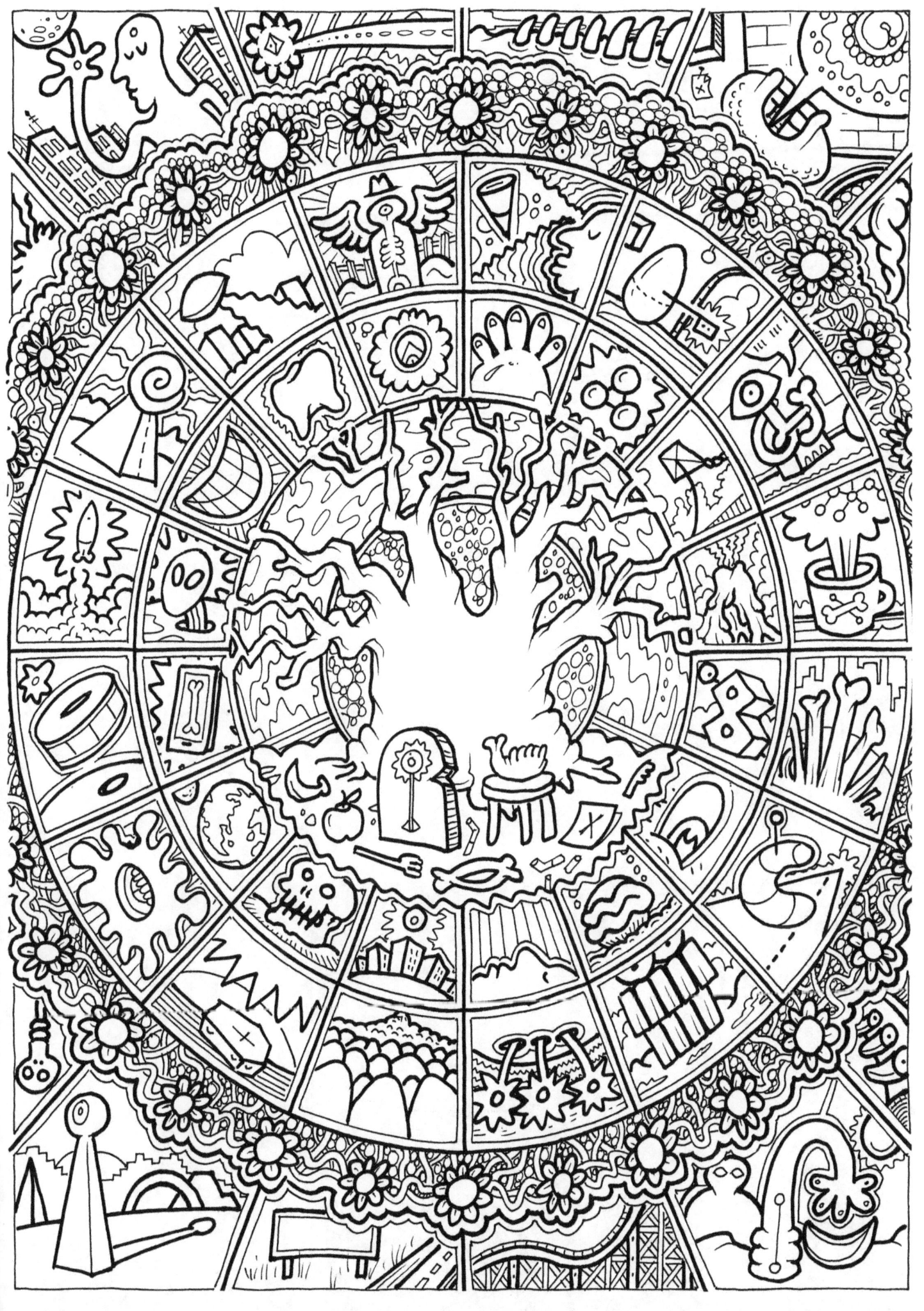

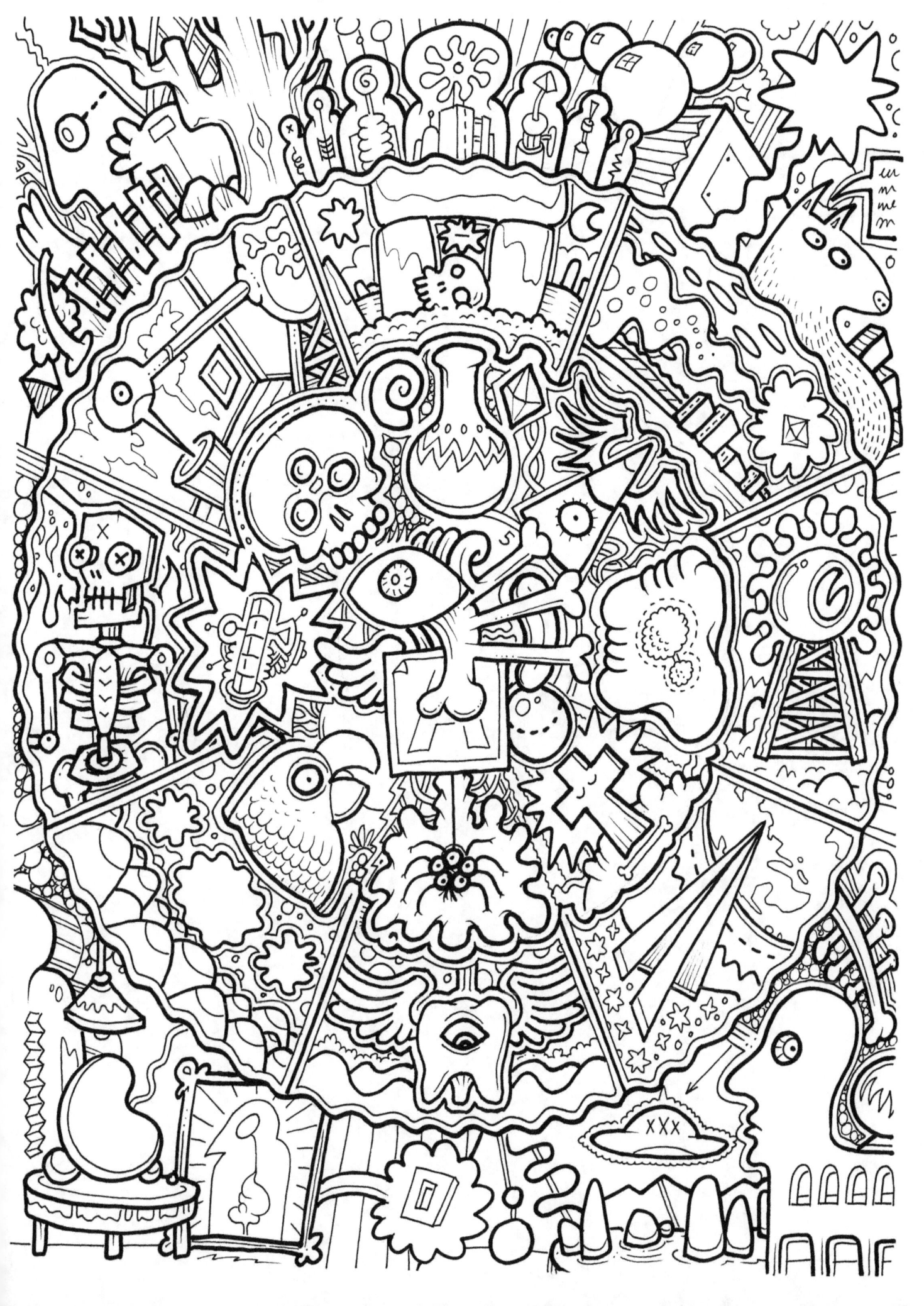

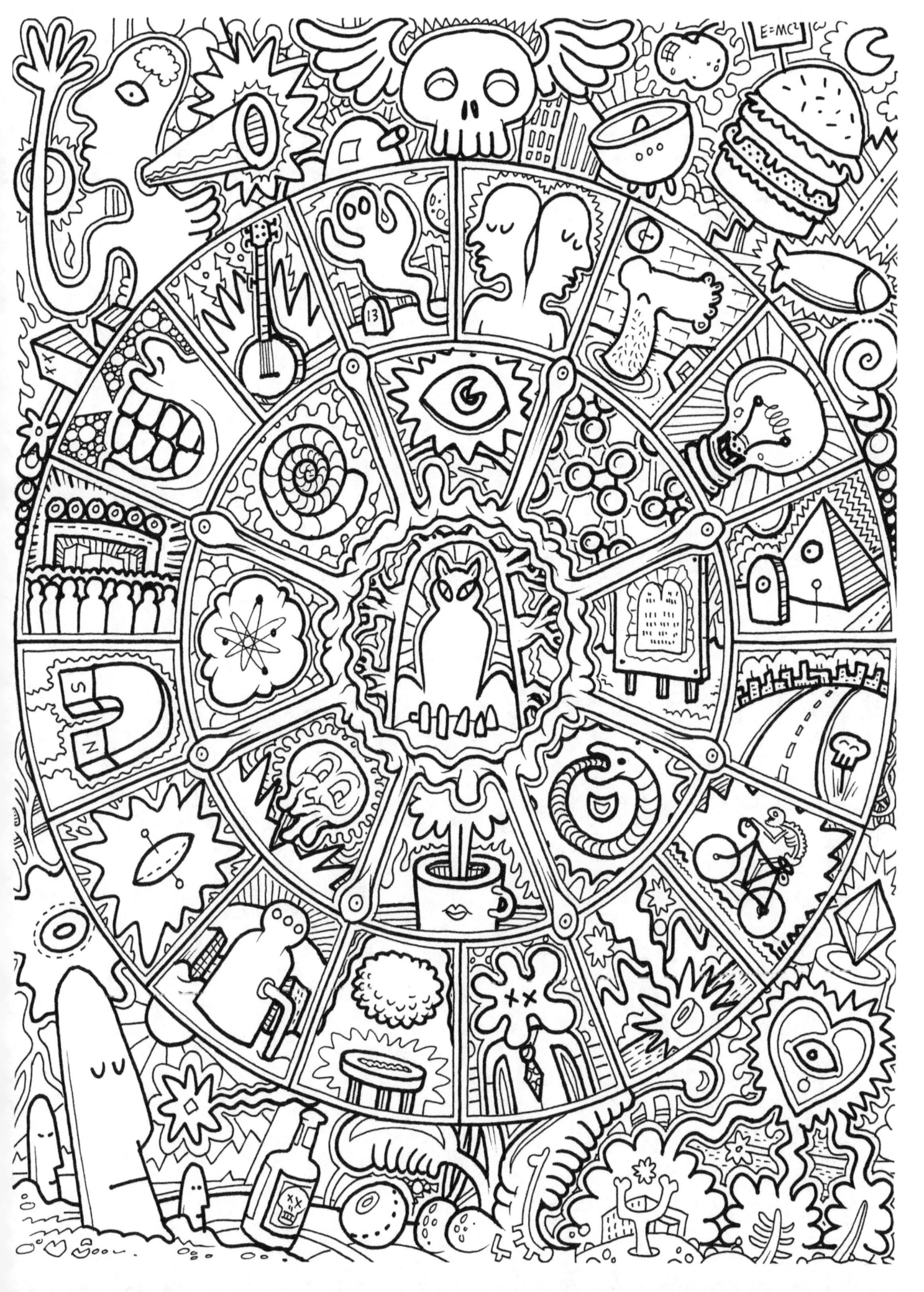

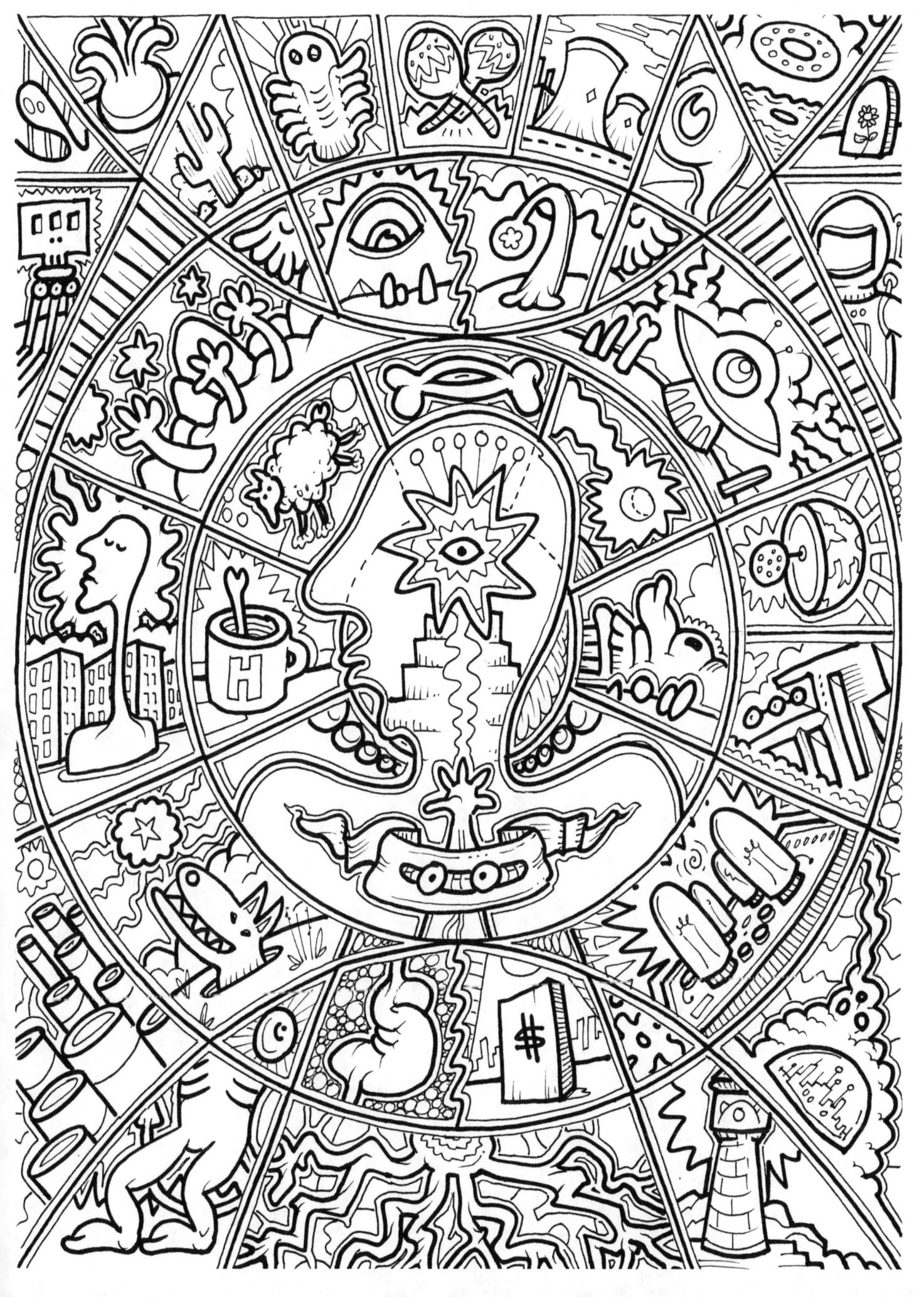

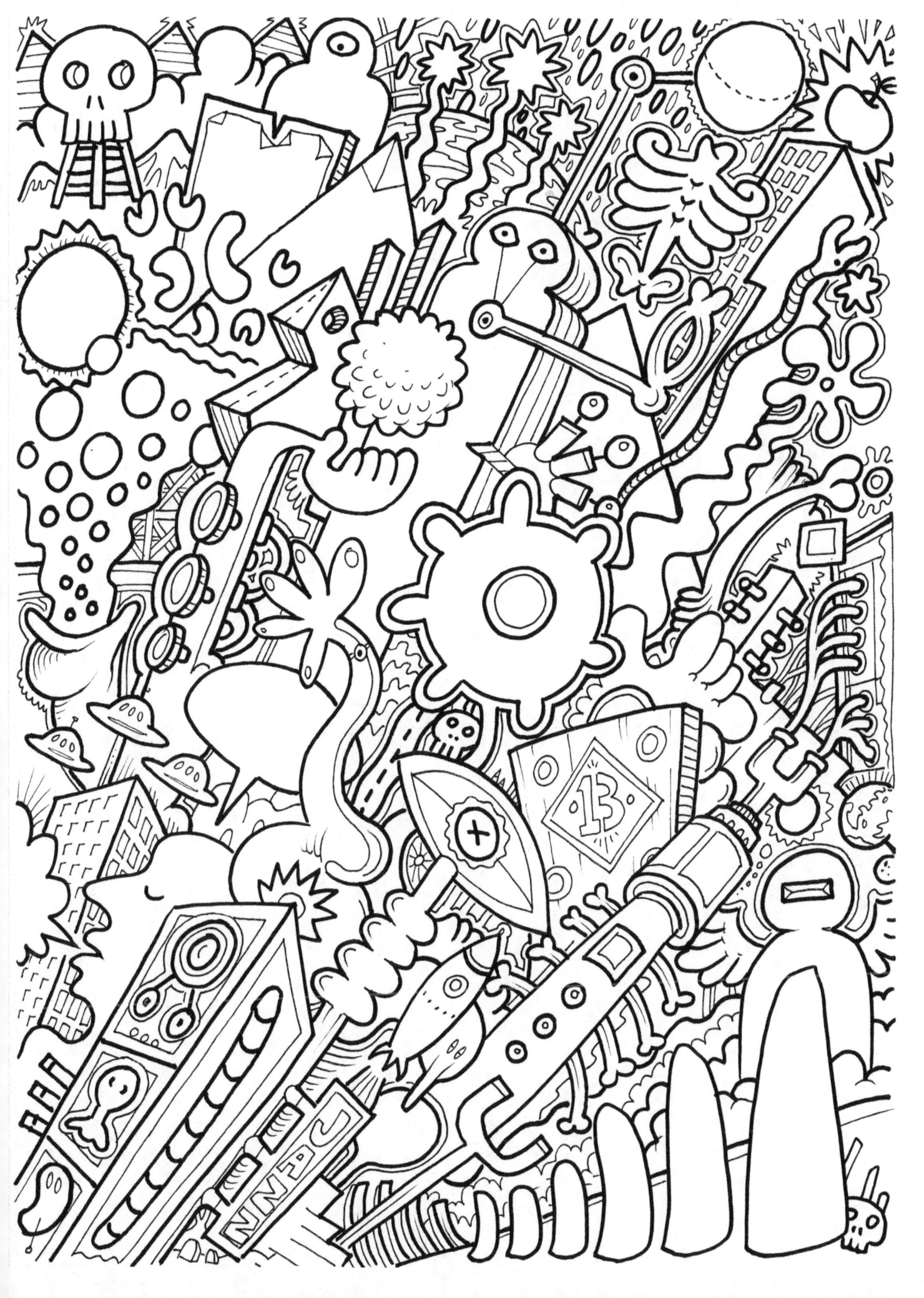

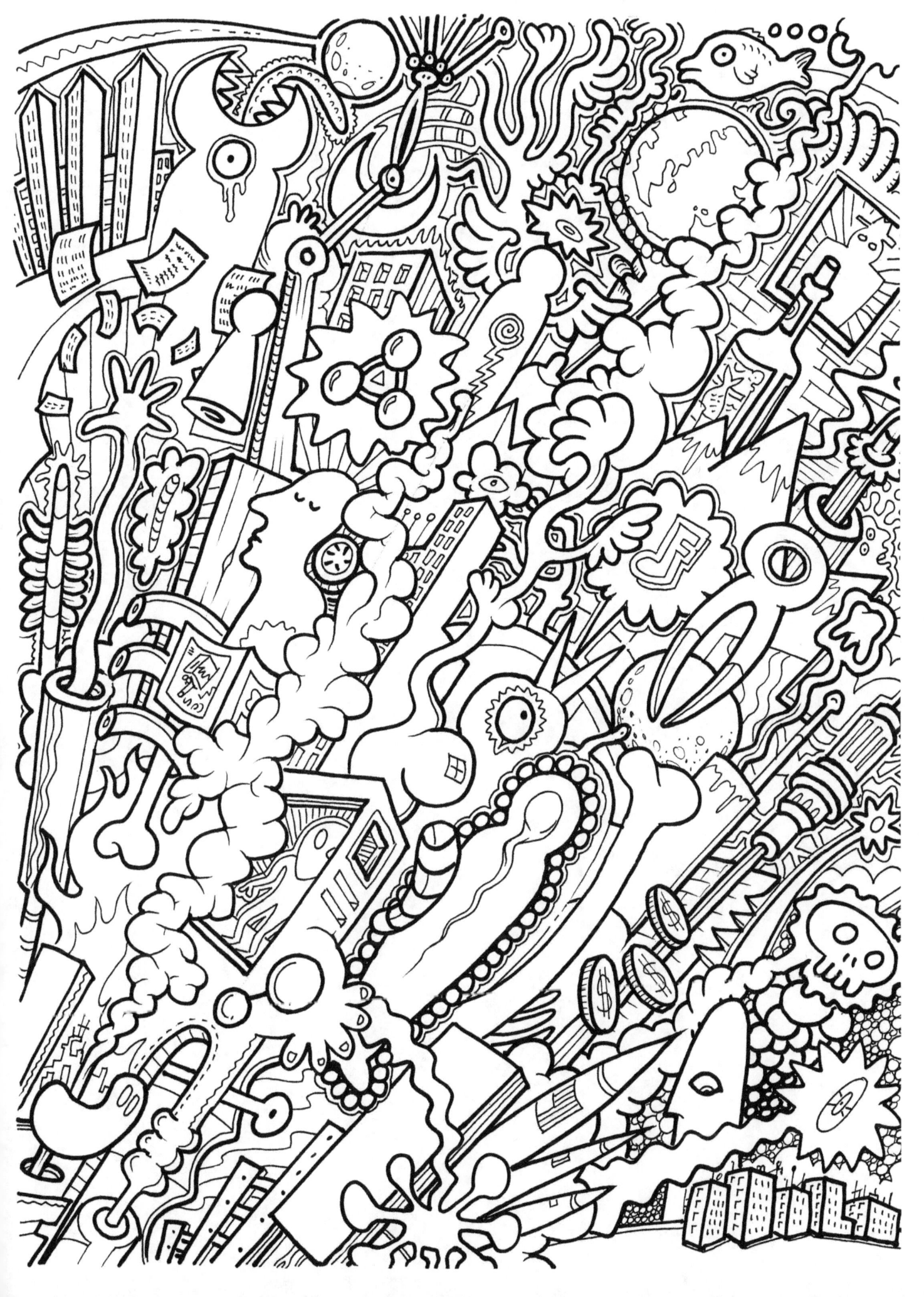

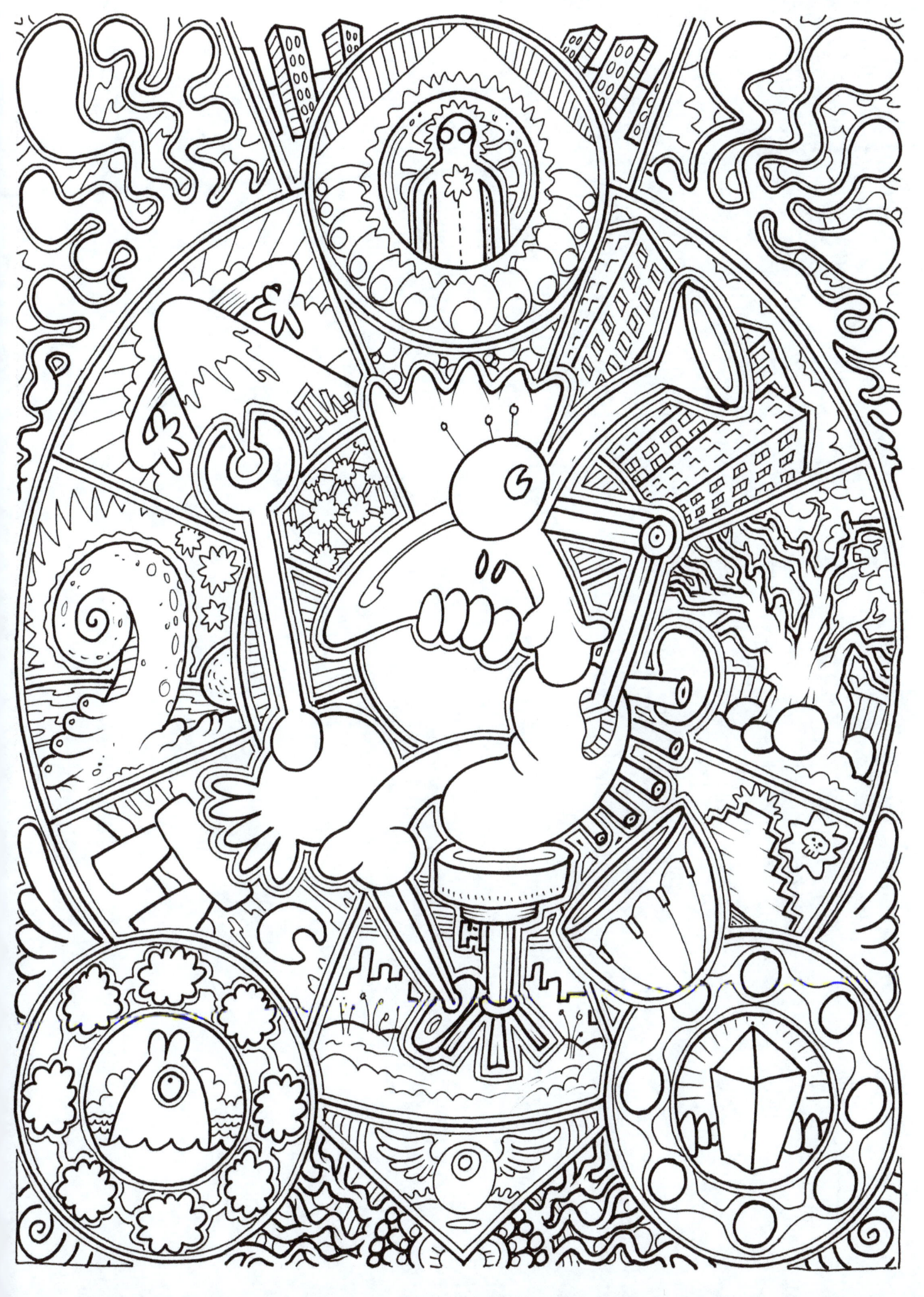

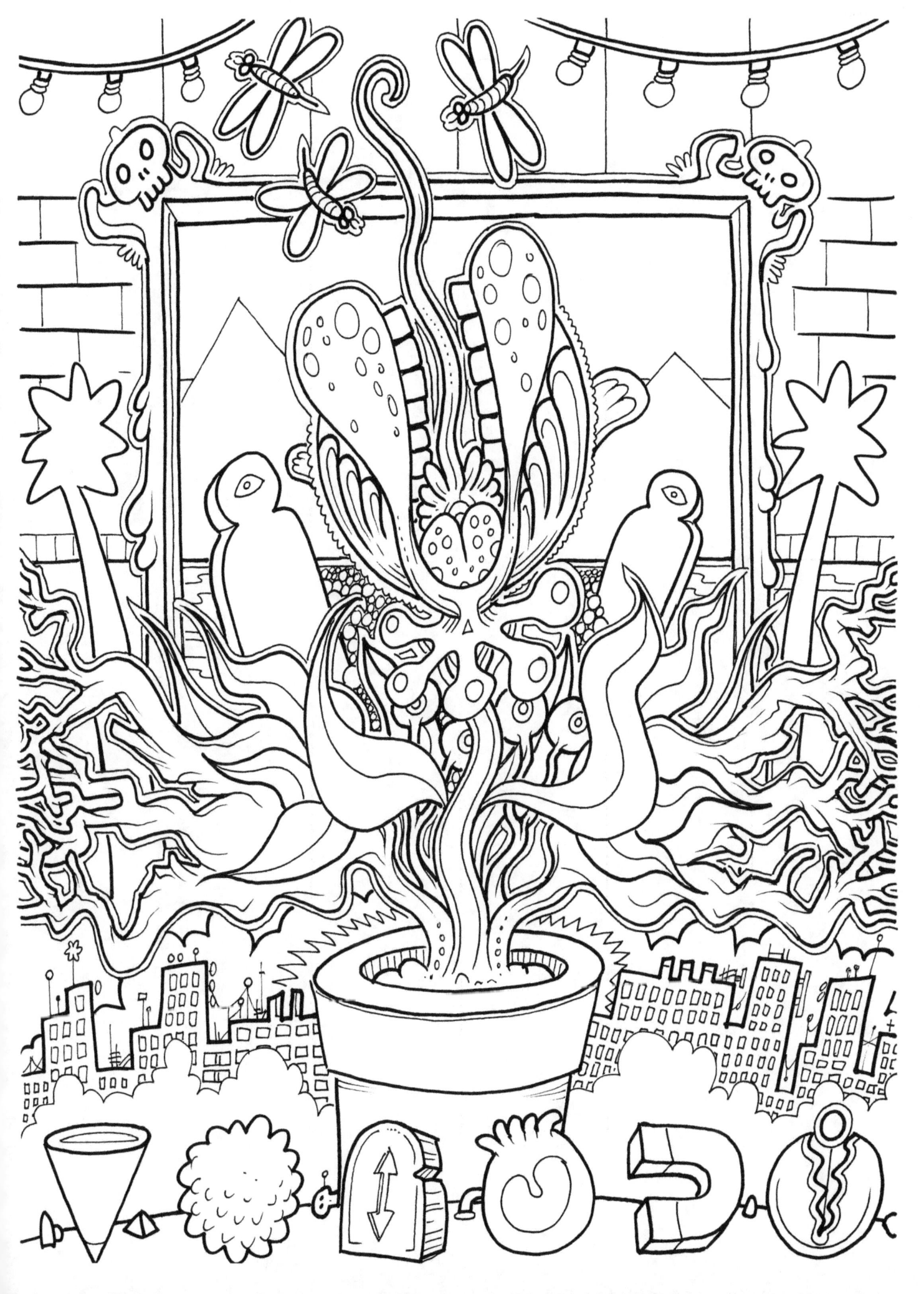

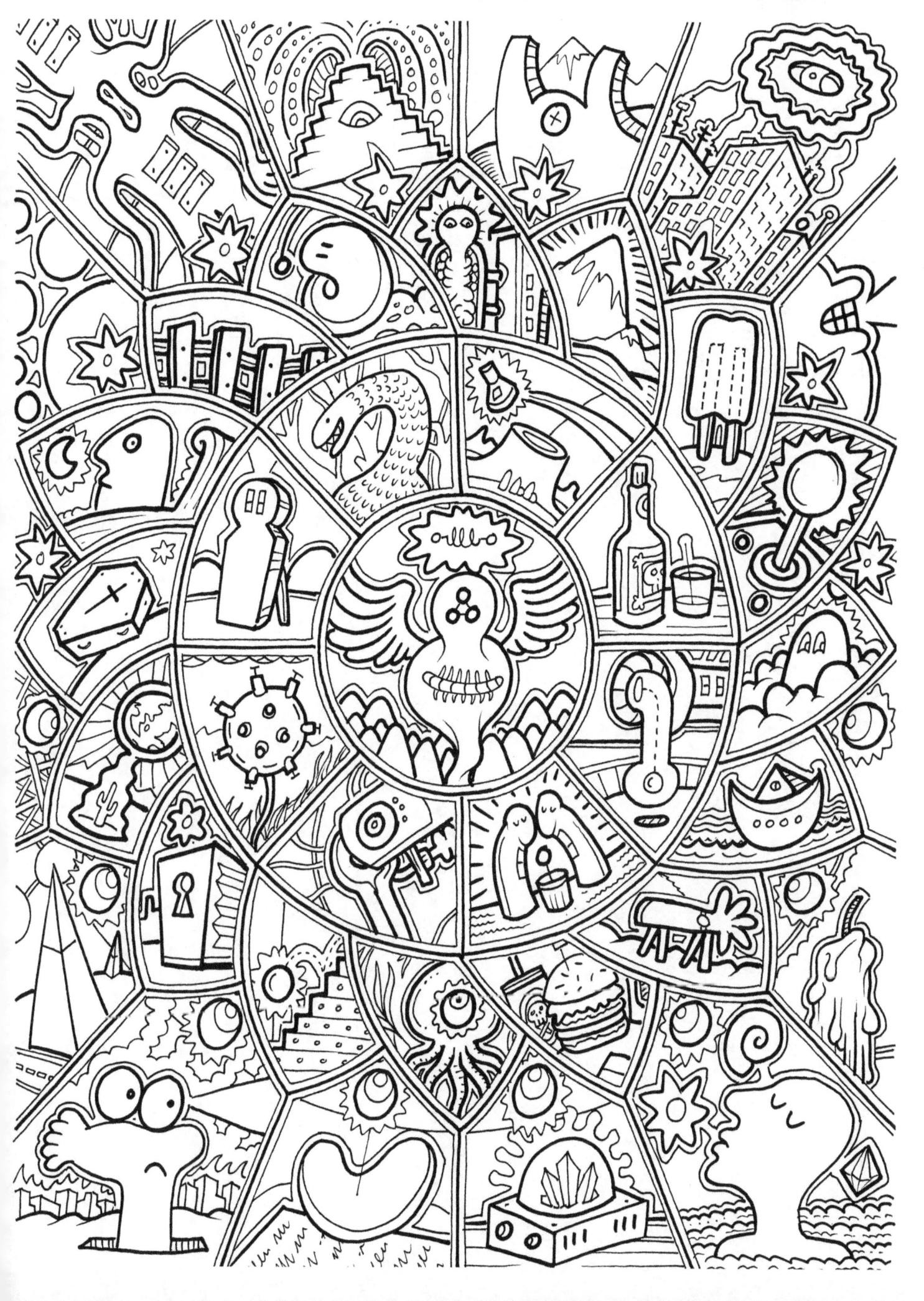

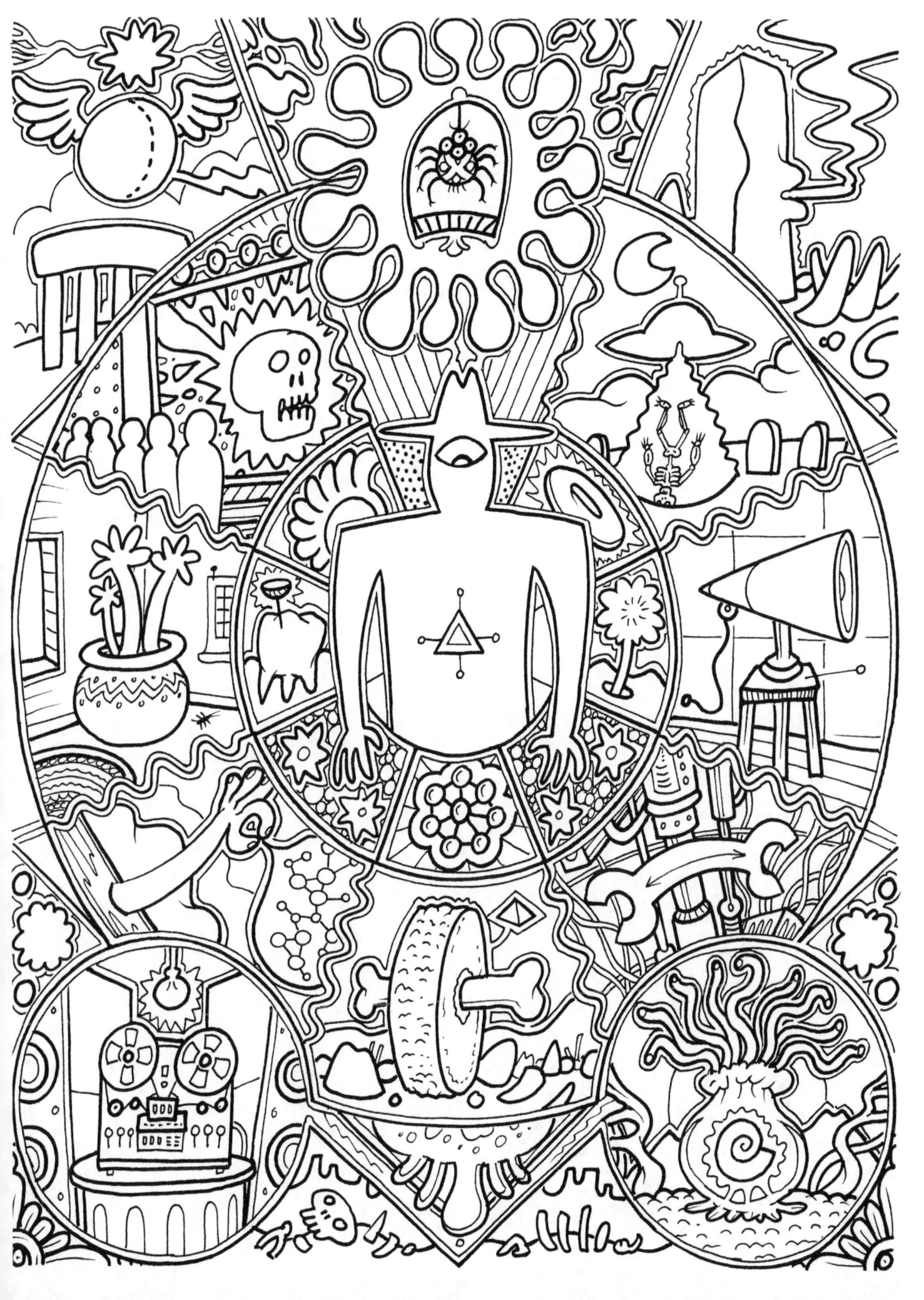

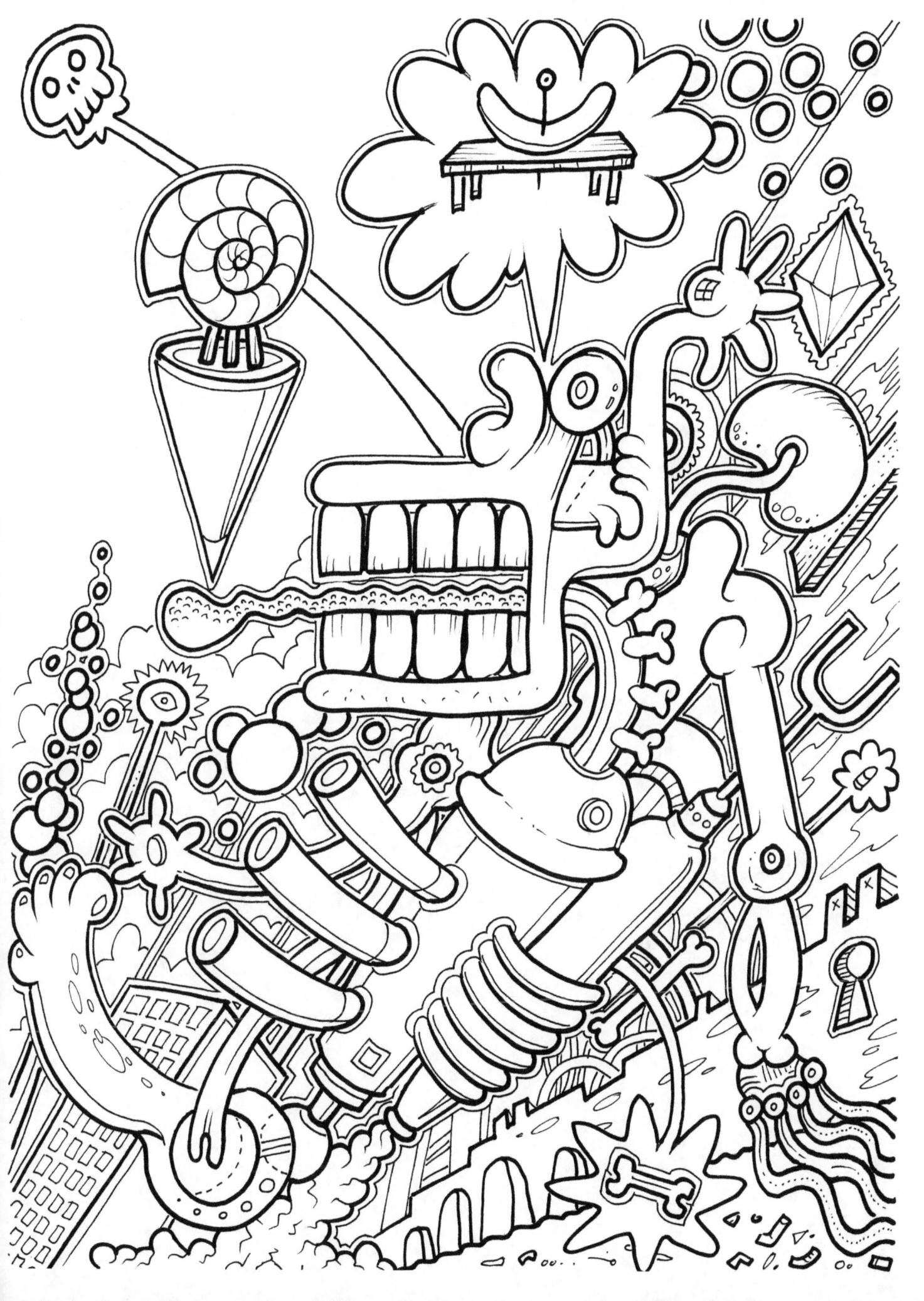

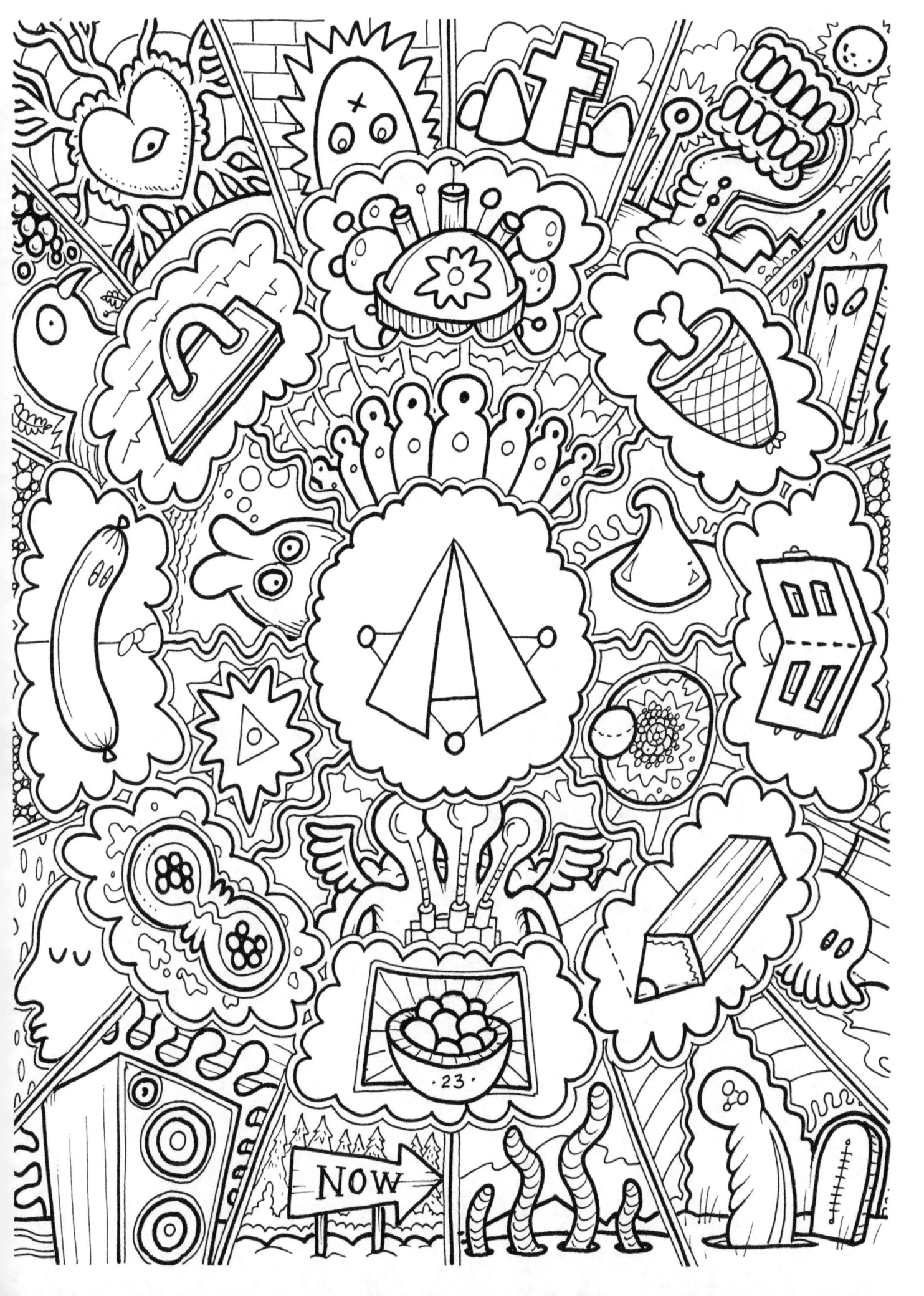

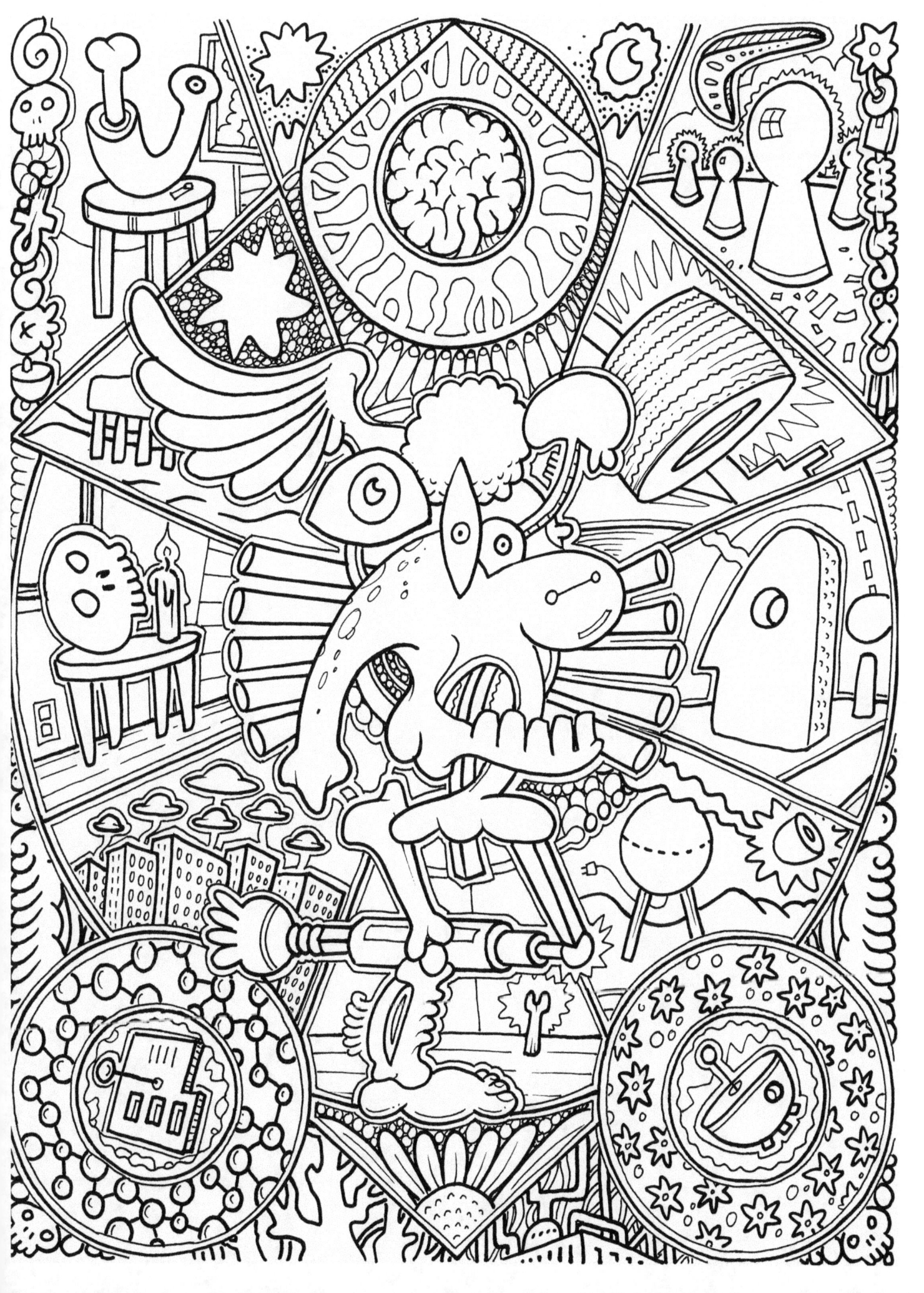

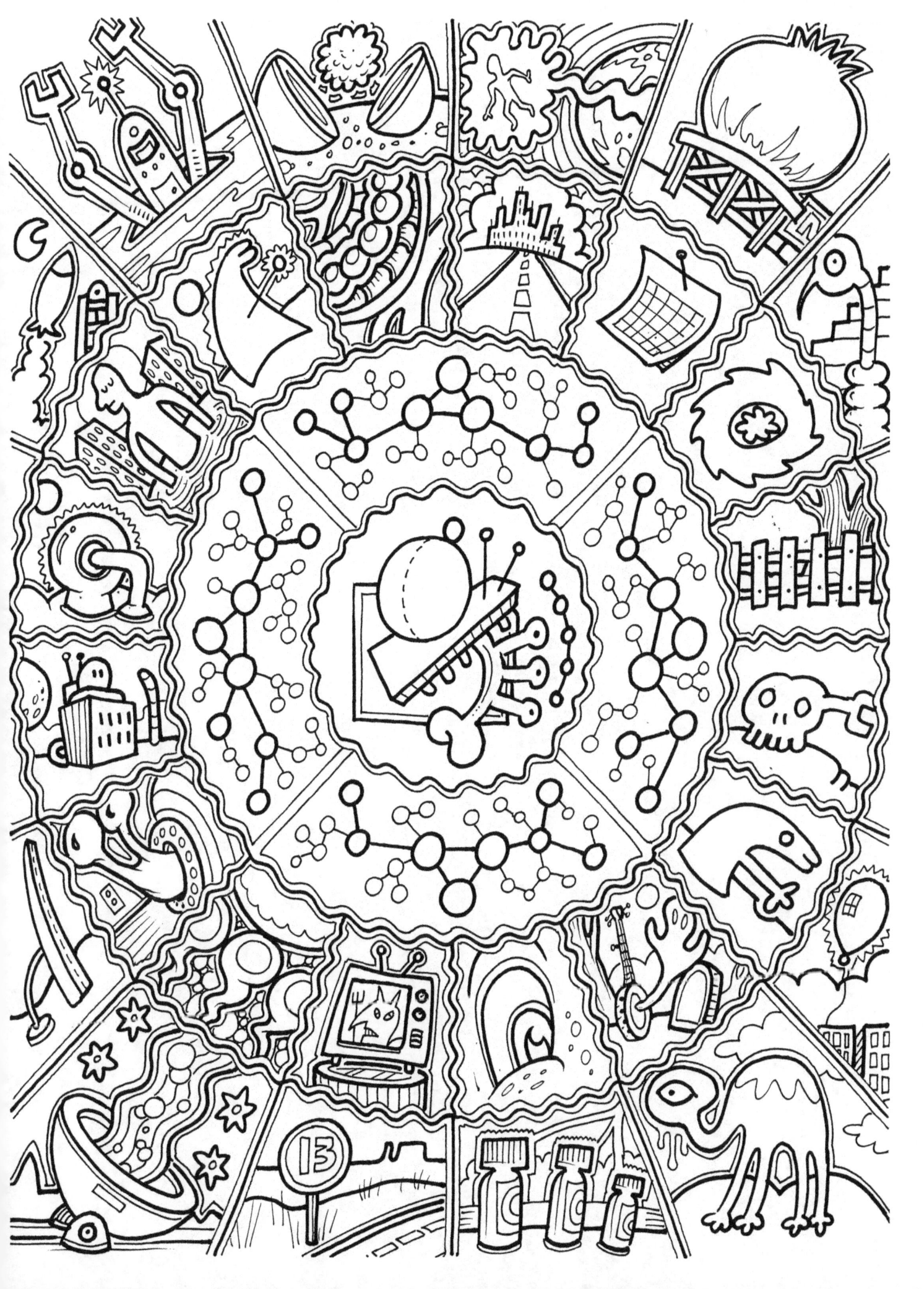

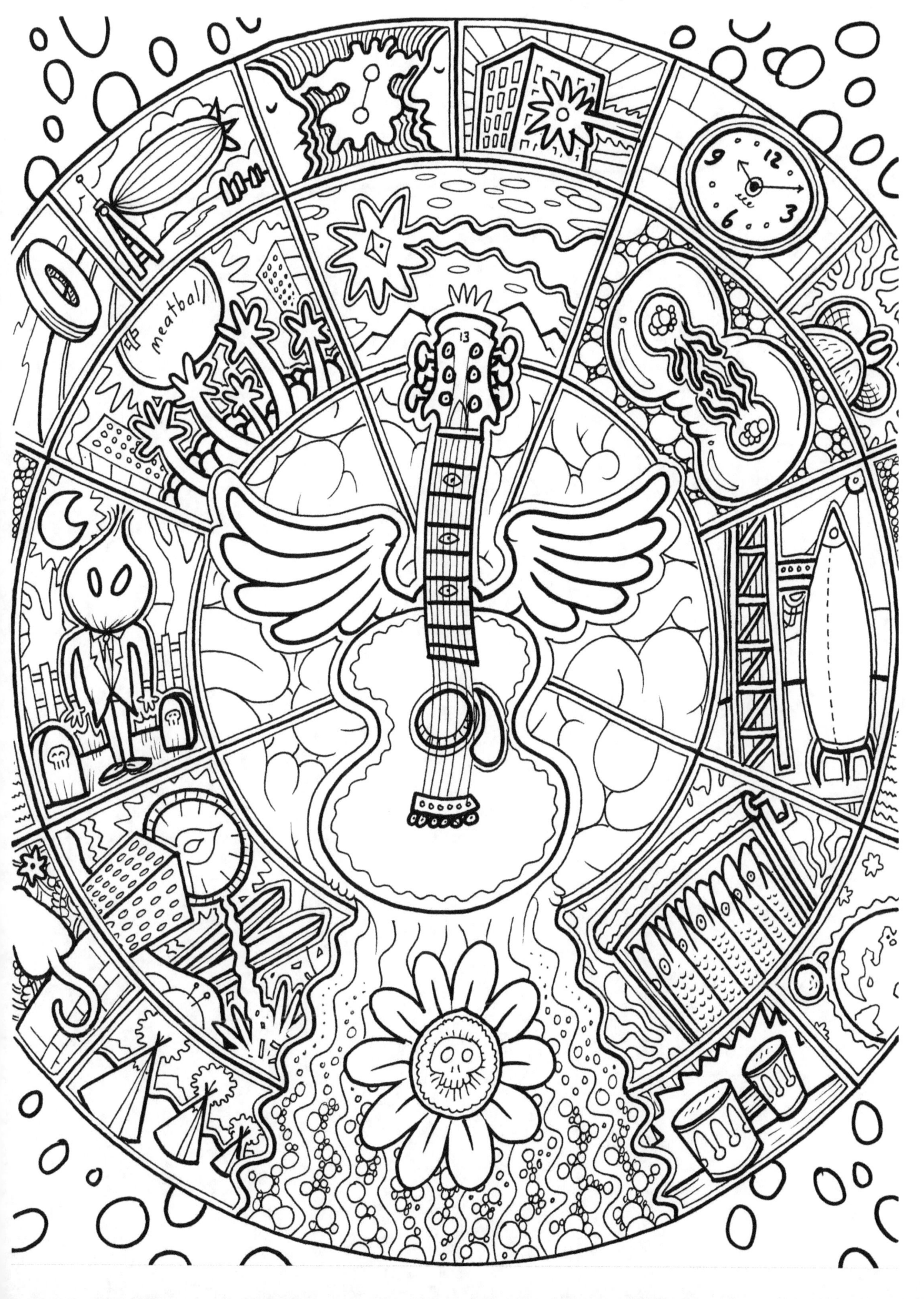

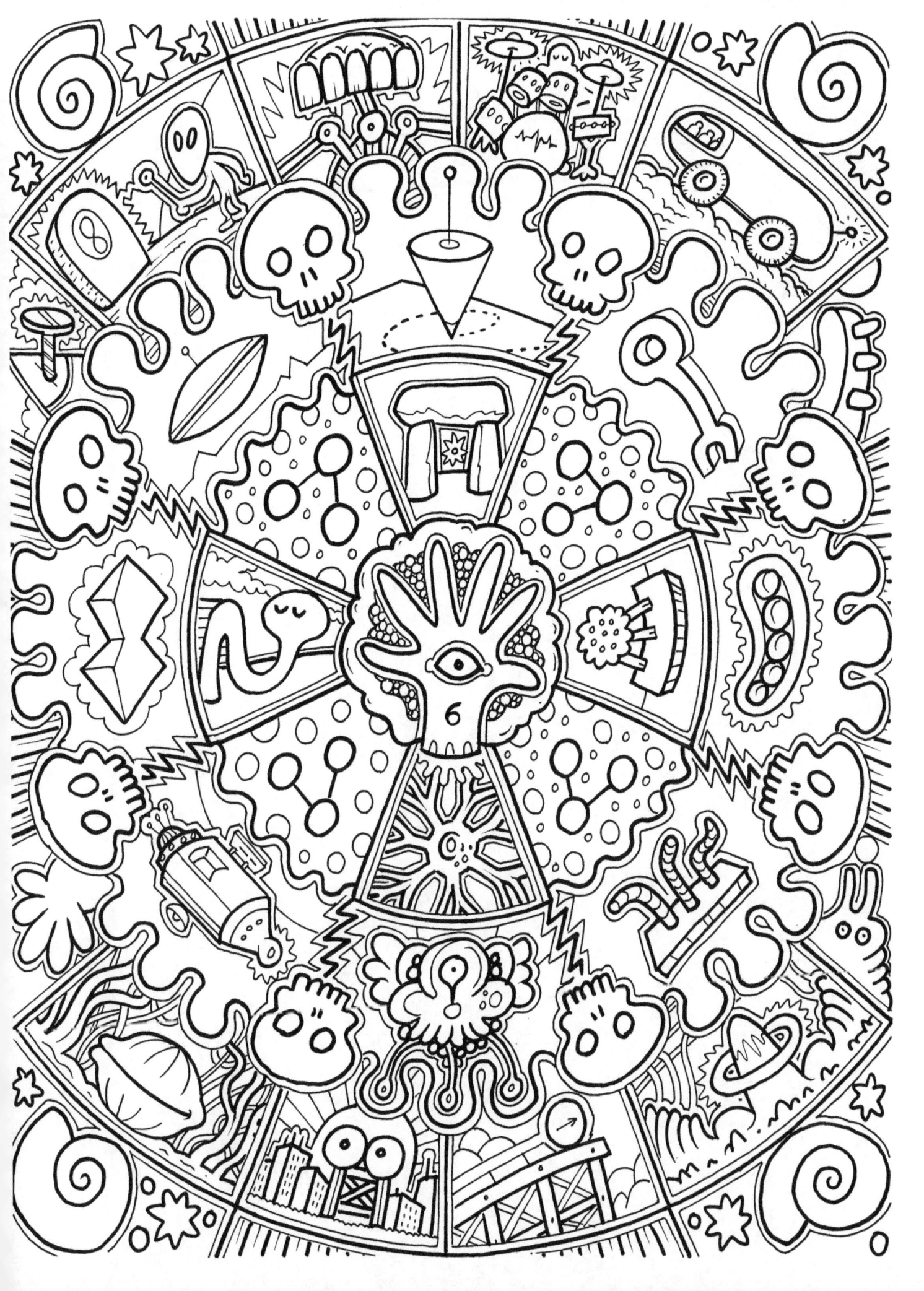

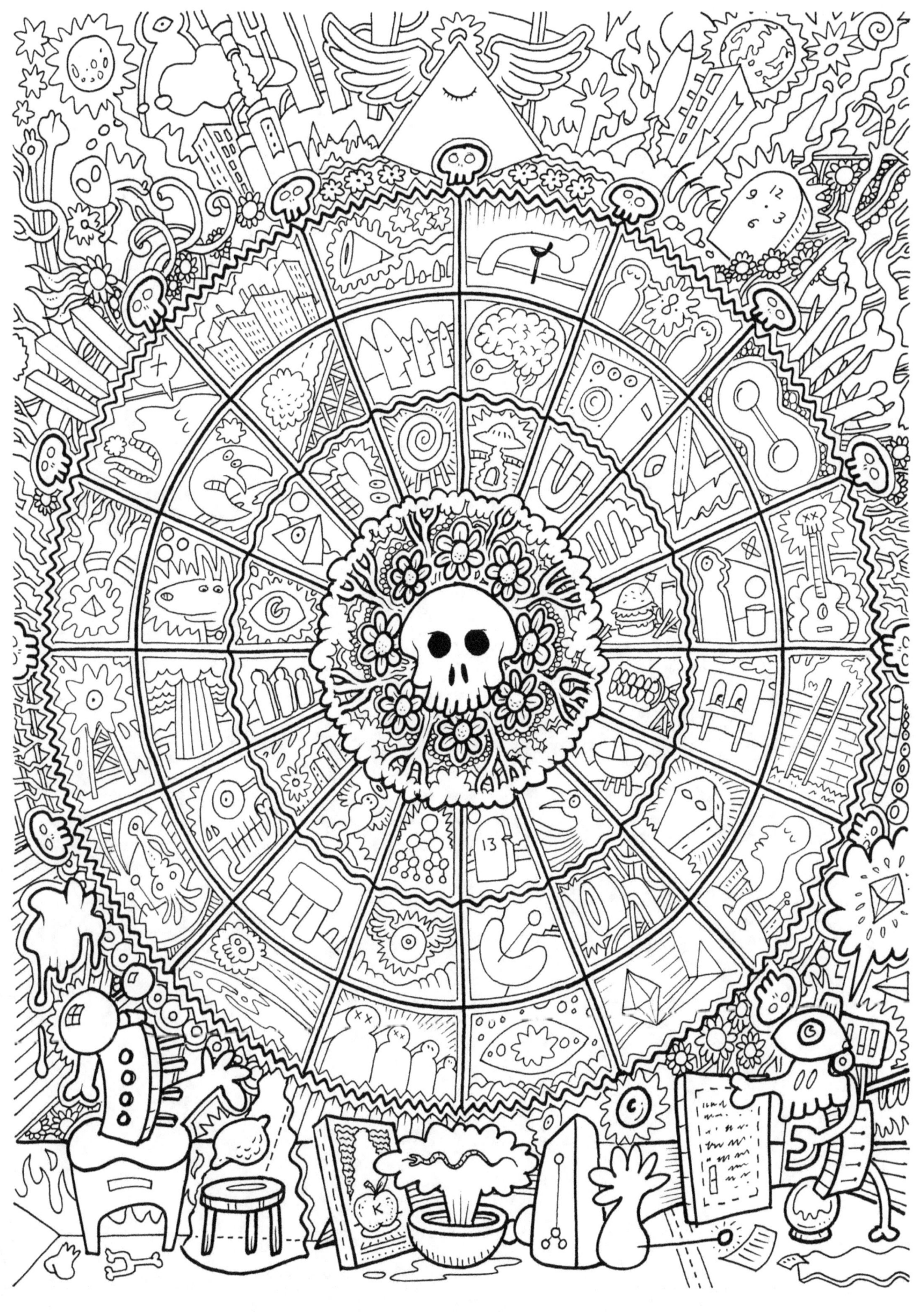